E BOOK™

Reptiles

ANN O. SQUIRE

Children's Press®
An Imprint of Scholastic Inc.
New York Toronto London Auckland Sydney
Mexico City New Delhi Hong Kong
Danbury, Connecticut

Content Consultant
Stephen S. Ditchkoff, PhD
Professor of Wildlife Sciences
Auburn University
Auburn, Alabama

Library of Congress Cataloging-in-Publication Data
Squire, Ann O.
 Reptiles / Ann O. Squire.
 pages cm.—(A true book)
 Audience: 9–12.
 Audience: Grade 4 to 6.
 Includes bibliographical references and index.
 ISBN 978-0-531-21755-9 (lib. bdg.) — ISBN 978-0-531-22340-6 (pbk.)
 1. Reptiles—Juvenile literature. I. Title.
 QL644.2.S735 2013
 597.9—dc23   2013000099

All rights reserved. Published in 2014 by Children's Press, an imprint of Scholastic Inc.
Printed in China 62
SCHOLASTIC, CHILDREN'S PRESS, A TRUE BOOK, and associated logos are trademarks and/or registered trademarks of Scholastic Inc.
1 2 3 4 5 6 7 8 9 10 R 23 22 21 20 19 18 17 16 15 14

Front cover: A baby panther chameleon catches a cricket.

Back cover: Green tea python

Find the Truth!

Everything you are about to read is true *except* for one of the sentences on this page.

Which one is **TRUE**?

T or F   Snakes and other reptiles have slimy skin.

T or F   Most reptiles can take care of themselves as soon as they hatch.

Find the answers in this book.

Contents

1 Land, Sea, and in Between

Do a snake, a sea turtle, and an alligator have anything in common? 7

2 Meet the Reptiles

What kinds of animals are reptiles? 15

3 Habitats and Food

Where do reptiles live? 25

THE **BIG** TRUTH!

Reptiles in Peril

Why are some reptile species in danger of dying out? 32

Baby sea turtles must make their way to the ocean quickly after hatching.

4 Communication and Reproduction

How do reptiles communicate with each other? . . . **35**

5 Reptiles and People

What should you do if you want to keep a reptile as a pet? **41**

True Statistics **44**

Resources **45**

Important Words **46**

Index **47**

About the Author **48**

The tortoise's round, stumpy legs are designed for walking on land.

CHAPTER 1

Land, Sea, and in Between

As the sun sets on the Arizona desert, a large rattlesnake lies hidden in a rock crevice. The brown and tan pattern on its back makes the snake almost impossible to spot against its rocky surroundings. Although the snake is motionless, it is alert and watchful. From time to time, it flicks out its forked tongue to test the air. Before long, the snake's patience is rewarded. A field mouse darts past where the rattlesnake is hiding.

 Each time a rattlesnake sheds its skin a segment is added to its tail.

Successful Catch

The mouse is fast, but the rattlesnake is faster. In an instant, the snake strikes. It sinks its fangs into the mouse's body and injects deadly **venom**. Then it waits. Within a few minutes, the venom has done its work. The rattlesnake opens its jaws wide and swallows the rodent headfirst. With the mouse bulging in its stomach, the snake slithers away to find a place to rest while digesting its meal.

Rattlesnakes are venomous from birth.

Green sea turtles often lay more than one nest of eggs in a single nesting season.

Turtle in the Sea

As waves break on a deserted Hawaiian beach, a female green sea turtle comes ashore. Trudging awkwardly through the sand, she reaches a spot above the high tide line, where the ocean cannot reach. Then she goes to work, digging a hole with her back flippers. When it is deep enough, she lays about 100 eggs, depositing them carefully into the hole.

Baby sea turtles must make their way to the water quickly to avoid being eaten.

The turtle covers the nest with sand and heads back out to sea. Baby turtles begin to develop inside the buried eggs, and after a couple of months, the babies hatch. After breaking out of their leathery shells, the hatchlings dig their way to the surface and head for the water. Except for the females that will come ashore to lay their own eggs in a few years, these turtles will spend their entire lives at sea.

Alligator in the Swamp

On a muddy riverbank deep in the Florida Everglades, an American alligator basks in the sun. Soon it inches forward, barely raising its body off the ground, and slides into the murky water. All that can be seen above the surface are the alligator's eyes and the tip of its long snout. The alligator is completely still and looks more like a floating log than an animal.

An alligator's eyes and nostrils stay above water so that it can watch for prey and breathe as it floats.

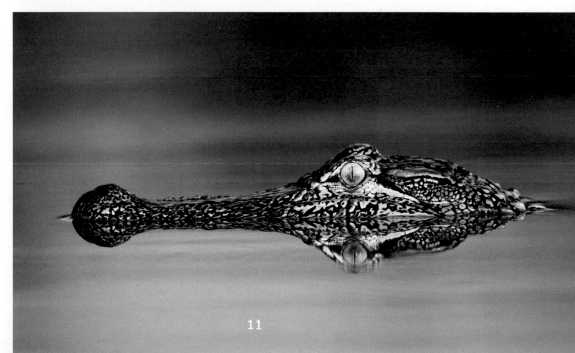

Suddenly, there is a quick movement. The water splashes and churns. The alligator raises its massive head. In its powerful jaws is a large fish, which thrashes wildly as it tries to escape. The alligator throws its head back several times, opening its jaws wide until the fish is in the right position. Then, with one giant gulp, the alligator swallows the fish whole.

An alligator uses its strong jaws and sharp teeth to catch and kill prey.

Some reptiles spend their entire lives in the water.

Same or Different?

At first glance, these three animals seem very different from one another. The rattlesnake lives on land, while the green sea turtle spends its entire life in the water. The alligator is comfortable on land or in the water. The alligator and the turtle each have four legs, while the snake has none. The snake and the alligator are both meat eaters, while the green sea turtle is a vegetarian, feeding on sea grass and algae. What can these three animals possibly have in common?

A giant leaf-tailed gecko makes itself look threatening when it feels that it is in danger.

14

CHAPTER 2

Meet the Reptiles

Although they live in different habitats, behave differently, and look very different from one another, snakes, turtles, and alligators have something in common. They are all reptiles. But what exactly is a reptile?

A reptile is a member of the animal class Reptilia. Within the class, there are different orders. Each order includes one or more families, which are made up of genera. Within each genus, there are a number of species.

There are almost 1,000 species of geckos in the world.

Reptile Orders

There are four orders alive today within the Reptilia class:

- Squamata, or snakes and lizards
- Testudines, or turtles and tortoises
- Crocodylia, or alligators and crocodiles
- Sphenodontida, or tuataras (a lizardlike reptile in New Zealand)

Snakes and lizards are by far the most numerous, with approximately 9,000 species. There are more than 300 species of turtles and tortoises, 25 species of alligators and crocodiles, and only 2 species of tuataras.

Tuataras look similar to their lizard cousins.

A turtle's shell is attached to its backbone, ribs, shoulders, and hips.

What Makes a Reptile a Reptile?

Like humans, reptiles are vertebrates. This means that they have a backbone. Reptiles, like most vertebrates, have a bony skeleton. Like us, reptiles have lungs and breathe air. We both have well-developed sense organs and sophisticated nervous systems. But that is where the similarities between humans and reptiles end.

A snake's scales can help it push itself forward across smooth ground.

Covered in Scales

Unlike humans' soft skin, reptile skin is made up of scales. The scales are usually tough and hard, to protect the animal from injury. A reptile's scales contain **keratin**, the same material in human fingernails. The scales are not individual plates, like a fish's scales. Instead, they are part of a continuous sheet of tissue. Reptile skin does not have sweat glands like human skin has. The skin of a lizard or snake is always smooth and dry.

Cold-Blooded

Reptiles are **ectothermic**, or cold-blooded. This means that a reptile's body temperature varies with its surroundings. If a snake is basking in the warm sun, its body temperature will be higher than if it is inside a cool, dark cave. Endothermic, or warm-blooded, animals such as humans, other mammals, and birds regulate their body temperature internally. A person's body temperature is always around 98.6 degrees Fahrenheit (37 degrees Celsius), whether that person's home is in Florida or Alaska.

A lizard basks in the sun to warm up.

Chameleon and other reptile eggshells are more flexible than bird eggshells.

Egg Layers

Most reptiles lay eggs. In that way, they are similar to birds. Reptile eggs usually have a leathery shell rather than a hard, brittle one. Reptile parents lay their eggs on dry land. The egg's tough shell protects the developing young. People sometimes confuse reptiles with frogs and other **amphibians**. One big difference is that the eggs of amphibians have soft shells and are laid in or near the water.

Miniature Adults

When they hatch, young reptiles look like smaller versions of their parents. This makes them different from amphibians, which go through an embryonic stage, such as when tadpoles turn into frogs. Mammals depend on their parents for care and feeding after birth, but most reptiles are independent as soon as they hatch. Some, like the green sea turtles, never even meet their parents.

This baby northern black racer hatched fully developed and ready to take care of itself.

Male or Female?

For people, a baby's sex depends on **chromosomes** that he or she inherits from the parents. In many reptiles, the hatchling's sex is determined by something else: temperature! This is true in all alligators and crocodiles, most turtles, and a few lizards. For some of these reptiles, low temperatures in the nest produce males. Higher temperatures produce females. For other species, the reverse is true. In some cases, one sex is produced in both high and low temperatures, and the other at temperatures in between.

Quick Facts About Reptiles

Group (number of species)	Diet	Reproduction	Distribution	Life Span
Snakes (Approximately 3,400)	**Carnivorous**	Most lay eggs; some species, including boa constrictor and green anaconda, give birth to live young	Found on every continent except Antarctica; also found in the sea	Some species live into their 20s or even their 40s
Lizards (Approximately 5,600)	Most small lizards eat insects; larger species may eat larger prey; some, like iguanas, are **herbivorous**	Most lay eggs, although some bear live young; some lizard species can reproduce without mating	Found on every continent except Antarctica	Small lizards live only a few years; larger species can live more than 20 years
Alligators, crocodiles, caimans, and gharials (25)	Carnivorous	All lay eggs; some protect their young after hatching	Found on all continents except Antarctica and Europe	45–100 years, depending on the species
Turtles and tortoises (300)	Most species are **omnivorous**, but some are carnivorous, and some herbivorous	All lay eggs	Found on every continent except Antarctica; sea turtles are found in all temperate and tropical oceans	Sea turtles live around 70 years; land tortoises live much longer, up to 150 years
Tuataras (2)	Carnivorous	All lay eggs	New Zealand	60–100 years

Black-collared snakes
are found throughout
the Amazon rain forest.

CHAPTER 3

Habitats and Food

Reptiles live in all types of habitats, from dry deserts to moist tropical rain forests, and from rivers and swamps to open oceans. Reptiles can be found on every continent except Antarctica. Many differences among reptiles can be explained by the fact that they live in such a wide range of environments. A reptile that makes its home in the desert will naturally have different characteristics and behaviors than a reptile that spends its life at sea.

Most snakes are not venomous.

Living in the Desert

Deserts are dry, so desert-dwelling reptiles have to conserve what little water they find. Gila monsters store water in the fatty tissue of their tails. A desert tortoise's bladder can store almost half the tortoise's body weight in water. By absorbing this stored liquid over time, the tortoise can go months without a drink.

Deserts have extreme temperatures. In cool weather, snakes and lizards sunbathe on rocks. In the summer heat, they retreat to rocky crevices or underground burrows.

A desert tortoise's body can store water in order to survive the dry desert.

A saltwater crocodile swims gracefully through the ocean waters near Palau, in the western Pacific.

A reptile's skin is impermeable, meaning water cannot pass through it.

Aquatic Reptiles

Alligators, crocodiles, and sea turtles are a few of the reptiles that spend part or all of their time in the water. All of these animals have the ability to hold their breath underwater for long periods of time. Sea turtles have strong, flattened flippers that allow them to move easily through the water. Alligators have a powerful tail to propel and steer them as they swim.

Komodo dragons sometimes eat carrion, or meat from dead animals they find.

Finding Food . . .

Most reptiles are carnivores. The bigger the reptile, the bigger the prey it can catch and eat. Small lizards feed mostly on insects. Larger lizards and snakes eat birds, mammals, and smaller reptiles. The Komodo dragon has been known to eat prey as large as water buffalo.

Some turtles and lizards are herbivores. Land tortoises eat grasses and plants, while most sea turtles feed on kelp and algae.

. . . And Eating It

Many reptiles swallow their food whole. For snakes, this is the only option. Snakes do not have limbs to help them break their food apart. Crocodiles and alligators may also swallow prey whole. For very large prey, the crocodile bites the animal and violently shakes its head to tear the prey into smaller pieces. This can be hard on a crocodile's teeth. Fortunately, if this reptile loses a tooth, a new one grows in its place.

A crocodile can grow as many as 3,000 teeth during its lifetime.

Hiding in Plain Sight

Most reptiles hunt other animals for food, so it helps if these **predators** can blend in with their surroundings. Many snakes and lizards have dull, blotchy markings that make them almost invisible when they're on rocks or in grass. Crocodiles and alligators have eyes and nostrils on top of their heads. They can stay almost completely underwater as they wait for prey animals to come by. Their eyes and nostrils stay above water so they can still see and breathe.

This bushmaster snake is well hidden among the brush on the forest floor.

Reptile World Distribution

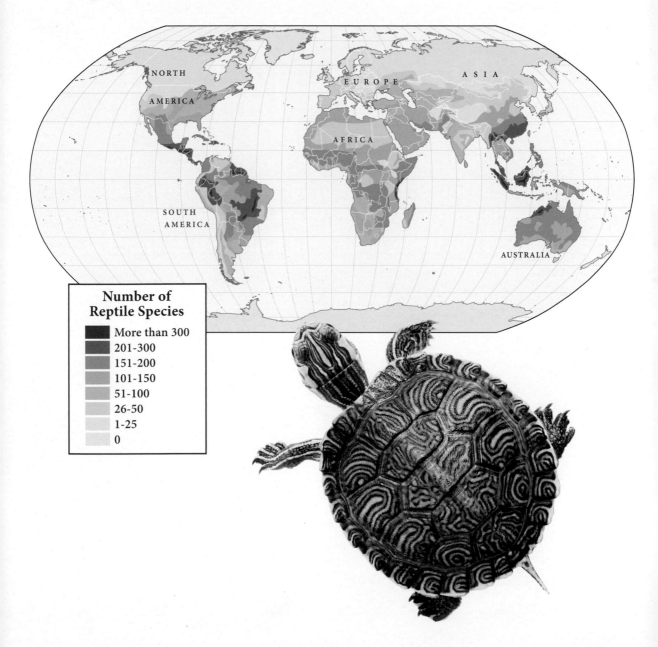

Number of Reptile Species

- More than 300
- 201–300
- 151–200
- 101–150
- 51–100
- 26–50
- 1–25
- 0

Reptiles in Peril

Many reptiles are secretive and difficult to study. Only about 17 percent of reptile species have been studied enough to determine whether a species is at risk. Of these, more than half are threatened or endangered.

Why are these animals in danger? Like all animals, reptiles are affected by human activities.

Humans often drain wetlands to build homes and factories and develop farmland. With nowhere to live, American crocodiles, bog turtles, and other wetland species could face extinction.

Marine reptiles such as sea turtles must cope with ocean pollution and accidental capture in fishing nets. Human disturbance of reptile nesting grounds and egg collection also threaten these animals.

In some areas, nonnative predators such as rats, cats, and dogs have had serious impacts on snake and lizard populations. Humans also kill reptiles for their skins, or collect and sell the animals as pets.

A male anole displays
its colorful throat sac.

CHAPTER 4

Communication and Reproduction

Like all animals, reptiles communicate with one another. Vision is one of the reptile's most important senses. These animals often communicate through visual signals such as color or movement. Many male lizards have brightly colored patterns on their sides or bellies to attract the attention of a mate. Male anole lizards attract females by puffing out their large throat sac. Male lizards also use bright colors, along with push-up displays, to announce ownership of their territory.

 Anoles change color in response to changes in light and heat.

Chemical Communication

Some reptiles rely on chemical signals to communicate. Among garter snakes, males and females look so similar that even the snakes cannot tell if one is a female or a male. During mating season, the females produce a **pheromone**. When a male approaches another snake, he flicks his tongue over that snake's body. If he detects the pheromone, he knows the snake is female and ready to mate. If the pheromone is not there, he knows the other snake is male and continues his search.

Male garter snakes are attracted to a female's pheromone during the spring mating season.

Alligators bellow with their mouths closed.

A male alligator's bellow causes the surrounding water to "dance," or vibrate.

Sound

Despite having no vocal cords, crocodiles and alligators often use sounds to communicate. Adult alligators cough, hiss, and bellow to threaten other alligators. They also bellow during mating season. Baby alligators make high-pitched sounds while still inside their eggs. In response, the mother sometimes helps them hatch by unburying the eggs and carefully cracking the eggshells with her teeth.

Alligators and other crocodilian species often provide more care to their young than other reptiles do.

Raising Young

For many years, people thought that most reptile parents were like the sea turtle, whose mothering job is done once she lays her eggs. But scientists are discovering that many reptile species do at least protect their babies after hatching. After crocodile babies hatch, the mother carefully picks up the tiny hatchlings in her mouth and carries them to the water. She stays with them and cares for them until they are about five weeks old.

Some snakes also take care of their babies. After laying her eggs, a python mother will coil her body around them, protecting them and keeping them warm for several months until they hatch. Rattlesnakes do not lay eggs, but instead give birth to live young. Rattlesnake mothers sometimes stay with their young for more than a week, until the baby snakes shed their skin for the first time.

An Angolan python mother wraps around its eggs.

An alligator swims in the pool of a
Florida apartment building.

CHAPTER 5

Reptiles and People

Reptiles in the wild are naturally wary of people and will usually try to avoid them. But as the human population grows, people sometimes move into areas that were once reptile habitat. This has been an issue throughout the southeastern United States, especially Florida, as people build homes, golf courses, and parks in alligator habitats. Alligators occasionally end up in backyard swimming pools. They may prey on pets and livestock.

 The biggest threat to alligators is habitat destruction.

Reptile Pets

Snakes and lizards are sometimes kept as pets. Before getting one, do some research. How big will the reptile grow? How long will it live? Make sure it was bred in captivity. What care does it need? Reptiles have different needs from dogs and cats. You can also take care of reptiles by becoming involved in organizations that protect them in the wild. These amazing animals are an important part of Earth's ecosystems. Helping reptiles also helps the planet.

Two or more green iguanas can live together with enough space. But this isn't true for all reptiles.

Python Problems

Burmese pythons are native to Southeast Asia. Some people in the United States have tried to keep them as pets. However, Burmese pythons grow to 7 feet (2.1 meters) or longer. Unable to care for these snakes, irresponsible pet owners sometimes release them into the wild.

In colder areas, released pythons cannot survive. But South Florida, especially near the Everglades, has tropical temperatures and plenty of food. Burmese pythons thrive there. They prey on bobcats, deer, and even alligators. As a result, many of Florida's native species have nearly disappeared. ★

True Statistics

Average weight of the saltwater crocodile, the world's heaviest reptile: 2,200 lb. (998 kg)

Length of the dwarf gecko, the world's smallest known reptile: 0.75 in. (1.9 cm)

Length of the longest snake in captivity: 25 ft. (7.6 m), a reticulated python

Average length of the Komodo dragon, the world's largest lizard: 10 ft. (3 m)

Age of the world's oldest living animal: 179 years, a giant land tortoise

Did you find the truth?

(F) Snakes and other reptiles have slimy skin.

(T) Most reptiles can take care of themselves as soon as they hatch.

Resources

Books

Daly, Timothy M. *Alligators*. New York: Children's Press, 2013.

Franchino, Vicky. *Sea Turtles*. New York: Children's Press, 2013.

Hutchinson, Mark. *Reptiles*. New York: Simon & Schuster Books for Young Readers, 2011.

McCarthy, Colin. *Reptile*. New York: DK Publishing, 2012.

Visit this Scholastic Web site for more information on reptiles:
★ www.factsfornow.scholastic.com
Enter the keyword **Reptiles**

Important Words

amphibians (am-FIB-ee-uhnz) — cold-blooded animals with backbones that live in water and breathe with gills when young; as adults they develop lungs and live on land

carnivorous (kahr-NIV-ur-uhs) — having meat as a regular part of the diet

chromosomes (KROH-muh-sohmz) — structures inside the nucleus of a cell that carry the genes that give living things their individual characteristics

ectothermic (ek-tuh-THURM-ik) — cold-blooded

herbivorous (hur-BIV-ur-uhs) — eating only plants

keratin (KAIR-uh-tun)—a protein that makes up hair, claws, nails, feathers, scales, and other animal parts

omnivorous (ahm-NIV-ur-uhs) — having a diet that contains both plants and meat

pheromone (FAYR-uh-mohn) — a chemical substance that is usually produced by an animal and serves as a signal to other individuals of the same species to engage in some kind of behavior

predators (PRED-uh-turz) — animals that live by hunting other animals for food

venom (VEN-uhm) — poison produced by some snakes, spiders, insects, and other creatures

Index

Page numbers in **bold** indicate illustrations

algae, 13, 28
alligators, **11–12**, 13, 15, 16, 22, 23, 27, 29, 30, **37**, **38**, **40**, 41, 43

babies, **10**, **21**, **22**, 37, **38**–39
births, 8, 21, 23, 39
body temperatures, **19**, 22, 26, 43
breathing, **11**, 17, 27, 30

carnivores, 23, 28
chromosomes, 22
colors, 7, **34**, 35
communication, **34**, 35, **36**, **37**
crocodiles, 16, 22, 23, **27**, **29**, 30, 33, 37, 38

ectothermic species, 19
eggs, **9**, 10, **20**, **22**, 23, 33, 37, 38, **39**
endangered species, 32–33
extinction, 33
eyes, **11**, 30

females, **9**, 10, 22, 35, **36**, 37, 38, **39**
flippers, 9, 27
food. *See* insects; plants; prey.

habitats, 7, 9, 11, **13**, 15, 23, **24**, 25, **26**, **27**, **31**, **33**, **40**, 41, 42, 43
herbivores, 23, 28
hunting, **11**–12, 30

iguanas, 23, **42**
insects, 23, 28

jaws, 8, **12**

males, 22, **34**, 35, **36**, **37**
map, **31**

markings, **30**
mating, 23, 35, **36**, 37, 42

nests, **9**–10, **22**, 33
nostrils, **11**, 30

orders, 16

people, 17, 18, 19, 20, 22, 32, 33, **40**, 41, 42, 43
pets, 33, 41, **42**, 43
pheromones, **36**
plants, 13, 23, 28
predators, **10**, 30, **33**
prey, 7, **8**, **11**, **12**, 23, **28**, 29, 30, 41, 43
pythons, **39**, **43**

rattlesnakes, **6**, 7, **8**, 13, 39
Reptilia class, 15, 16

sea turtles, **9–10**, **13**, 21, 23, 27, 28, **33**, 38
senses, 7, 17, 35, 36
shedding, 7, 39
skin, 7, **18**, 27, 33, 39
species, 15, 16, 22, 23, 32, 33, **38**
swallowing, 8, 12, 29
swimming, **11**, **27**, **40**

tails, 7, 26, 27
teeth, 8, **12**, **29**, 37
threatened species, 32–33
tortoises, 16, 23, **26**, 28
tuataras, **16**, 23
turtles, **9–10**, **13**, 15, 16, **17**, 21, **22**, 23, 27, 28, **33**, 38

venom, 8, 25

About the Author

Ann O. Squire is a psychologist and an animal behaviorist. Before becoming a writer, she studied the behavior of rats, tropical fish in the Caribbean, and electric fish from central Africa. Her favorite part of being a writer is the chance to learn as much as she can about all sorts of topics. In addition to writing *Reptiles*, *Mammals*, and *Birds* in Scholastic's True Book series, Squire has written about many different animals, from lemmings to leopards and cicadas to cheetahs. She lives in Katonah, New York.